Window Stars

Thomas Berger

Window Stars

Making folded stars from colored papers

HearthSong

Translated from Dutch by Polly Lawson

Photographs and design by Ernst Thomassen
Illustrations by Ronald Heuninck

First published in 1996 by Floris Books
Thirteenth printing 2008

ISBN 978-086315-245-8

Printed in Poland

General Instructions

The Paper

Transparent stars are made by folding each piece of transparent paper into a single star-point and then assembling these single star-points to make a star.

To make transparent stars use kite-paper or tissue-paper.

— *Kite-paper (transparency paper)* is sufficiently transparent and is more robust than translucent tissue-paper, so it is more easily worked. It is available in 6–8 colors and in two sizes: about 27^1/2″ × 19^1/2″ (70 × 50 cm) and about 40″ × 27^1/2″ (100 × 70 cm).

— *Tissue-paper* is less color-fast than kite-paper and since transparent stars are usually left to hang for a long time, tissue-paper stars can quickly lose their color in sunlight. It is available in 15–20 colors, in various sizes.

The Colors

When choosing the colors remember that the pattern in the transparent stars emerges from the different layers of paper laid upon each other. In the more complicated star-points there can be up to eight layers of paper and light can hardly shine through. Do not use dark colours for complicated stars or the pattern will not be discernible. Yellow, orange, light green and pink are the most suitable.

Size

Do not make the stars too small as it is harder to fold them exactly. The diameter of the transparent stars shown in this book depends on the size of the sheets as well as on the manner of folding. Most of the stars have a diameter of 8″ (20 cm). Where the diameter for a particular star is different this is indicated.

By altering the length and/or width of the sheets you will alter the pattern. Examples of this are given in Figures 36 and 39 where the width of the sheets is 3″ (7.5 cm) and 1^3/4″ (4.5 cm) respectively.

The Sheets

To make the star-points we can begin with either square or rectangular sheets.

With square sheets the diagonal determines the dimensions of the star. A sheet of, for instance, 3″ × 3″ (7.5 × 7.5 cm) has a diagonal of a little over 4″ (10 cm). The

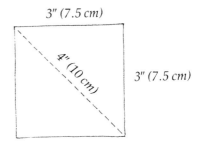

3″ (7.5 cm)

4″ (10 cm)

3″ (7.5 cm)

Figure 1

diameter of the star is twice the length of the points, that is about 8″ (20 cm).

With rectangular sheets (for instance 4″ × 3″, 10 × 7.5 cm) it is the length of the sheet which determines the dimensions of the star. Thus the diameter of the star will be 8″ (20 cm), that is, twice 4″ (10 cm).

Cutting out the sheets

Work out beforehand how many pieces can be obtained from one large sheet, as this avoids waste.

In this book we shall work with 3″ × 3″ (7.5 × 7.5 cm) squares and 4″ × 3″ (10 × 7.5 cm) rectangles. For more complicated stars it is advisable to use larger sizes.

Take great care that all the cut-out pieces are exactly the same size. To make squares of 3″ × 3″ (7.5 × 7.5 cm) cut out a piece 12″ × 12″ (30 × 30 cm) with a very sharp knife as accurately as possible.

From this piece sixteen sheets can be cut out in the following way: fold the piece in two with a very sharp crease. Cut through the crease with a very sharp knife. Fold these two halves in two and cut again. Repeat the process until you have sheets 3″ × 3″.

Folding

It is important to fold the sheets as exactly as possible because any divergence is magnified in the final result.

The crease must be really sharp. When the same points have to be folded twice (as in Figure 6) then do not make the first fold come exactly to the centre-line but allow a tiny space (about $1/32$″, 1 mm) in between. Ensure that the sides come exactly together with the second fold.

Stick all the folded pieces together with a little transparent glue, adhesive or glue-stick. Non-transparent adhesive becomes visible immediately when the star is hung up.

Sticking the pieces together

Turn the star-points over. It is easier to apply the glue to the smooth side and you will cause less damage to the folds. The second star-point is almost always stuck to the diagonal of the first, the third to that of the second, and so on.

Stick the stars to a window with a few small strips of double-sided adhesive tape, sticking them to the parts where the star is least transparent so that the tape will not show.

The Pattern

You can experiment as you fold the transparent stars. Indeed many of the stars in this book came about by just trying out one more fold. In order to see if a new way of folding will bring about a surprising result you do not need to make the whole star — it is enough to stick together five star-points. With less you will not see how the pattern repeats itself.

Finally it is intriguing to see with which colors the star turns out best.

Stars from squares

1. Simple eight-pointed star (Figure 3)

MATERIALS
8 squares 3" × 3" (7.5 × 7.5 cm)

METHOD
Generally stars made from squares have the diagonal as the central fold.
    Follow these steps:

1. Fold the sheets across the diagonal so that points B and C meet. Unfold again (Figure 2a).
2. Fold sides AB and AC inwards to lie along the diagonal (Figure 2b). Stick them down with a spot of glue. Fold all the star-points in this way.
3. Stick the star carefully together, sticking the unfolded bottom (D) of the second star-point to diagonal of the first (Figure 2c). Continue in this way until all the star-points have been stuck together.

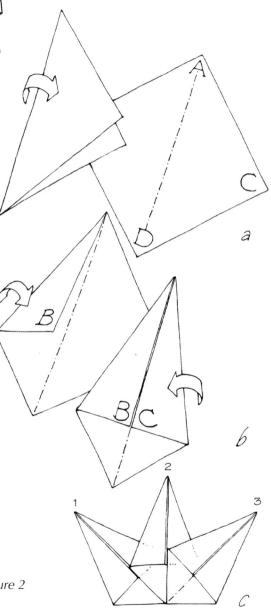

Figure 2

2. Ten-pointed star (Figure 5)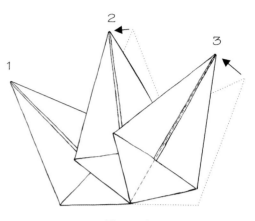

MATERIALS
10 squares 3″ × 3″ (7.5 × 7.5 cm)

METHOD
Fold the star-points in the same way as with the eight-pointed star (stages 1 and 2). Then stick the star together by sticking the unfolded bottom of the second star-point a little bit over the diagonal of the first (Figure 4). In this way the pattern of rays in the heart of the star is formed.

Figure 4

Figure 3

Figure 5

3. Eight-pointed star (Figure 7) ⬦ 𝅭

MATERIALS
8 squares 3″ × 3″ (7.5 × 7.5 cm)

METHOD
The eight-pointed star on page 8 was simple to fold. A slight alteration in folding will change the motif of the star. For example at the second stage make an extra fold opening the two flaps with the points B and C again and divide them into two, then fold them in again and stick them down (Figure 6). Stick the star together as in stage 3 on page 8.

4. Five-pointed-star (Figure 8) ⬦ 𝅭

MATERIALS
5 squares 3″ × 3″ (7.5 × 7.5 cm)
(The diameter of the star about 7″, 18 cm)

METHOD
By taking five instead of eight folded points you can make an interesting modification in the pattern of the star no. 3. In Figure 8 you can see that the overlap of each individual point is much less than half (as in Figure 2c) but only a fraction (in our example the overlap is about $1/2$″, 10–12 mm). In this way a pattern of rays appears in the middle.

Figure 7

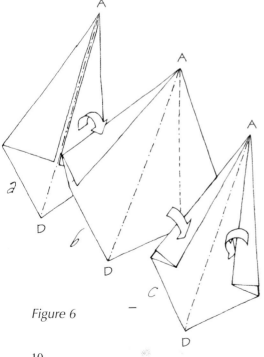

Figure 6

5. Ten-pointed star (Figure 9)

MATERIALS
10 squares 3″ × 3″ (7.5 × 7.5 cm)

METHOD
To obtain a ten-pointed star, double the number of points of the five-pointed star (no. 4). In this way a beautiful pattern will appear.

There are two ways of developing a ten-pointed star from a five-pointed one. The simplest way is to make two five-pointed stars and stick one on top of the other.

A more accurate result is obtained by first making a five-pointed star and then sticking the next five points one by one between the points of the first star.

Figure 8

Figure 9

6. Sixteen-pointed star (Figure 11)

MATERIALS
16 squares 3″ × 3″ (7.5 × 7.5 cm)

METHOD
Proceed from the folded star of Figure 2b on page 8, then make a further step by folding the two bottom sides in to the diagonal as shown on Figure 10. Open up the bottom sides and then fold the two side-flaps again into two and then in to the diagonal again. Because of this extra fold the width of the folded star-points is halved so that we need twice as many (16) star-points to make a star. Turn the star over so that point *D* comes to the outside and point *A* goes to the centre

Figure 10

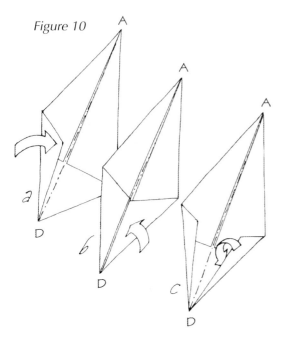

of the star. Stick the side of the second star-point along the diagonal of the first, and so on. On the outside a beautiful sun with rays is produced.

7. Ten-pointed star (Figure 12)

MATERIALS
10 squares 3″ × 3″ (7.5 × 7.5 cm)

METHOD
Fold the star-points according to the stages in Figure 10 and then stick them together in such a way that the points *A* point outwards and points *D* come to the centre. In this way a star is formed which is quite different from star no. 6.

Figure 11

Figure 12

Figure 13

13

As is to be seen in Figure 12 the folded-over bottom halves of the separate star-points are not stuck over each other along the diagonal but stuck to the folded-over sides.

Thus a ten-pointed star is formed with a bright circle in the middle and ten rays out from the centre.

As soon as you depart from the set number of eight or sixteen star-points, it will require some experimenting to determine how far the points will have to come over each other. At first use only a very little glue so that you can unstick the points easily.

8. Eleven-pointed star (Figure 13) ⬙ ⚲

MATERIALS
11 squares 3″ × 3″ (7.5 × 7.5)

METHOD
In star no. 3 on page 10 only the top side A is folded (Figure 6). The unfolded bottoms of the points were stuck to the diagonal of the preceding star-point, and so the heart of the star became darker in color (Figure 7).

In star no. 7 (Figure 12) the star-points are partly stuck over each other again and in this way the heart gets a pattern of rays.

With this eleven-pointed star a fresh fold is added to the stages shown in Figure 6. Fold the bottom star-points along the diagonal (Figures 14a and b) and stick them down. The star-points have now become narrower. Fold together eleven instead of

ten separate points and stick them together to make a star. In this way a special pattern is formed.

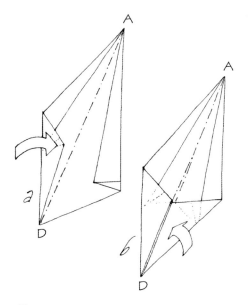

Figure 14

Stars from squares

9. Eight-pointed star (Figure 16)

MATERIALS
8 squares 4″ × 4″ (10 × 10 cm)
(The diameter of star: about 6″, 15 cm)

METHOD
These stars are of a different kind from those of the last chapter. The points are not sharp but have an angle of 90°. We now take larger pieces because some of the star-points need an extra fold.

Proceed as follows:

1. Fold each piece once over the diagonal so that point *B* covers point *C*, then unfold again (Figure 15a)
2. Repeat with points *A* and *D*.
3. Divide half of the diagonal *AD* into two equal parts to make point *E*. The distance *AE* is a quarter of the whole diagonal (Figures 15a and b).
4. Fold bringing point *D* up the diagonal *DA* to *E* (Figure 15b).
5. Fold sides *FB* and *FC* inwards along the diagonal (Figures 15c and d) and stick them together with a bit of glue.
6. Apply some glue to the back and stick side *FG* of the second star-point to the diagonal of the first, and so on (Figure 2c).

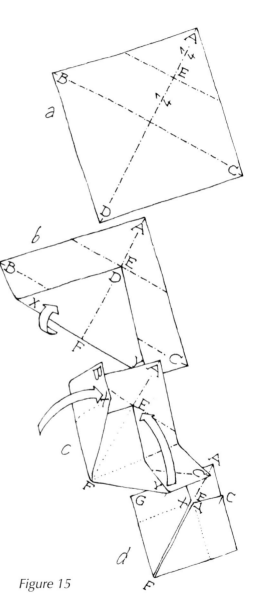

Figure 15

10. Eight-pointed star (Figure 18)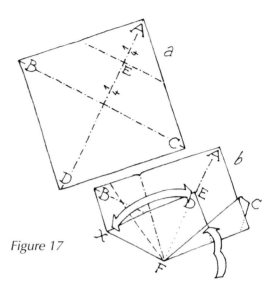

MATERIALS
8 squares 4″ × 4″ (10 × 10 cm)
(The diameter of star about 6″, 15 cm)

METHOD
Follow stages 1 to 4 as described for star no. 9 (Figure 15). Now fold the sides *FX* and *FY* inwards and then open them out again. Fold the outer edge of the two side-flaps inwards once more (Figure 17). Stick them down.

Stick each star-point along the diagonal of the preceding star-point.

Figure 17

Figure 16

Figure 18

Figure 19

11. Eight-pointed star (Figure 21)

MATERIALS
8 squares 4″ × 4″ (10 × 10 cm)
(The diameter of star about 6″, 15 cm)

METHOD
In stage 3 of star no. 9 (Figure 15) we divided the upper half of the diagonal *AD* into two equal parts giving point *E*. Now divide the distance *AE* into two equal parts giving point *F* (Figure 20a).

Fold bringing point *D* up the diagonal to *F*. Fold the sides *GX* and *GY* inwards and open them out again. Fold the two side-flaps in two inwards (Figure 20b). Stick them down.

Stick each star-point along the diagonal of the preceding star-point.

12. Six-pointed star (Figure 19)

MATERIALS
6 squares 4″ × 4″ (10 × 10 cm)
(The diameter of star about 6³/4″, 17 cm)

METHOD
Make the same star-points as for star no. 10, but now do not stick the points along the diagonal but stick them a little over each other. Slide the points under each other to find out how far the star-points should overlap each other.

Figure 21

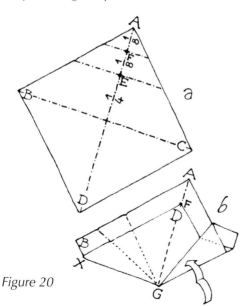

Figure 20

18

Stars from squares

13. Eight-pointed star (Figure 23)

MATERIALS
8 squares 4″ × 4″ (10 × 10 cm)

METHOD
For this series of stars, rather larger pieces will be used because all the variations which follow have an extra fold.

For this star proceed as follows:

1. First fold the pieces in two and then open them out again (Figure 22a).
2. Turn the pieces round a quarter turn and fold them again across.
3. Fold the points of the square to the middle (Figure 22b) to make the square *ABCD*. Open the points out again.
4. Halve the triangles which have appeared and fold them again to the middle. (Figure 22c). This leaves a hollow diamond in the middle.
5. Finally fold points *B* and *C* to the centre-line and that completes the star-point.
6. Stick the second star-point against the diagonal of the first, and so on (Figure 2c).

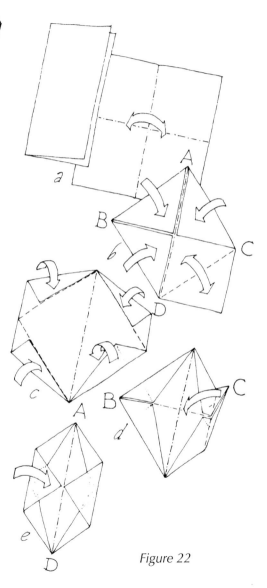

Figure 22

Figure 23

14. Eight-pointed star (Figure 25)

MATERIALS
8 squares 4″ × 4″ (10 × 10 cm)

METHOD
For this star follow the first five stages of star no. 13 (Figure 22). Figure 24 shows how to do the next step so that you get a pointed star-point on one side; fold the sides at the top to the vertical diagonal and stick them together.

Then stick the star together with the sharp points outwards. Stick the second star-point to the diagonal of the first, and so on (Figure 2c).

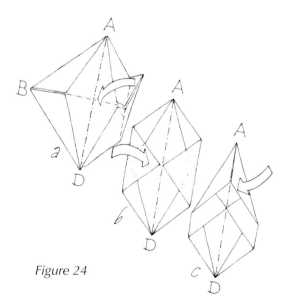

Figure 24

Figure 25

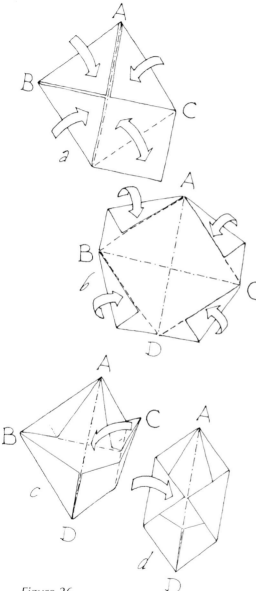

Figure 26

15. Eight-pointed star (Figure 27)

MATERIALS
8 squares 4″ × 4″ (10 × 10 cm)

METHOD
This star is again a variation of star no. 13, which is made by altering stage 4.

Figures 26b and c show how the lower two triangles are halved in a different way. Fold the triangles inwards and then fold points *B* and *C* again to the centre-line (Figure 26d).

Here too you make the star by sticking the second star-point along the diagonal of the first, and so on (Figure 2c). Now a completely different pattern appears inside the star.

Figure 27

Figure 28

16. Eight-pointed star (Figure 30)

MATERIALS
8 squares 4″ × 4″ (10 × 10 cm)

METHOD
This star is a variation of star no. 15.

Fold the star-points as described in star no. 15, but do not fold points *B* and *C* to the centre-line. Instead fold sides *AB* and *AC* to the vertical diagonal to make a sharp star-point (Figure 29b).

Stick the star-point of the second star with the sharp point outwards along the diagonal of the first, and so on. Figure 30 shows how the heart of the star remains the same as that of star no. 15 but that now a new pattern has come about in the outer part of the star.

VARIATION
You will get a surprising result if you stick one star on top of another. Figure 1 on page 6 shows a combination of star no. 6 and star no. 16.

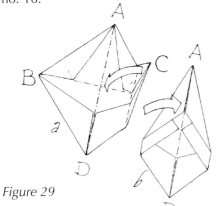

Figure 29

17. Six-pointed star (Figure 28)

MATERIALS
6 squares 4″ × 4″ (10 × 10 cm)
(The diameter of star about 5³/₄″, 17 cm)

METHOD
Make the same kind of star-points as for star no. 16, but instead of eight make only six. Stick the star-points at the bottom a little bit over each other. Try out how far the star-points should overlap each other to obtain the right proportions. A new open pattern is now formed in the heart of the star.

Figure 30

23

18. Eight-pointed star (Figure 32)

MATERIALS
8 squares 4″ × 4″ (10 × 10 cm)

METHOD
Follow the first 4 steps of star no. 13. After stage 4 turn the square round a quarter turn. The hollow diamond which in Figure 22d is vertical, now becomes horizontal (Figure 31a). Now fold, instead of points B and C, points A and D to the inside (Figure 31b). This produces a totally different pattern.

Stick the star-points together by sticking the second on to the diagonal of the first, and so on (Figure 2c).

19. Eight-pointed star (Figure 34)

MATERIALS
8 squares 4″ × 4″ (10 × 10 cm)

METHOD
With this star too follow the first four steps of star no. 13 and turn the square a quarter turn. Then fold points A and D to the centre but now so that the lines AB and BD lie along the diagonal BC (Figure 33).

Stick the star-points together by sticking the second on to the diagonal of the first, and so on (Figure 2c).

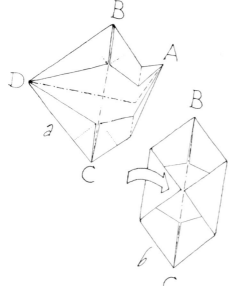

Figure 31

Figure 32

24

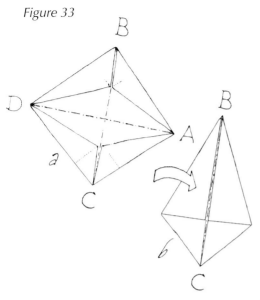

Figure 33

20. Sixteen-pointed star (Figure 35)

MATERIALS
16 squares 10 × 10 cm

METHOD
For this star fold sixteen star-points as described in star no. 19. But instead of point *B* stick point *C* in the centre of the star. Because this star-point is narrower than point *B*, double the number of star-points will be required.

Stick the star-points together by sticking the second on to the diagonal of the first, and so on (Figure 2c). A beautiful sun will appear.

Figure 34

Figure 35

Stars from rectangles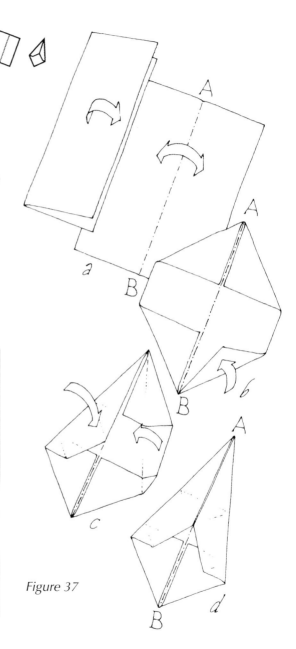

21. Simple eight-pointed star (Figure 36)

MATERIALS
8 rectangles 4″ × 3″ (10 × 7.5 cm)

METHOD
With stars of rectangles the long centre-line is the central fold.
   Proceed as follows:

1. Fold over the pieces lengthwise and open them up again (Figure 37a).

Figure 36

Figure 37

2. Fold the four corners inwards to the centre-line to make a point at the top and bottom (Figure 37b). Stick the corners down with a bit of glue.
3. Fold from the top point A the two sides again to the centre-line (Figure 37c). This sharp point forms one of the points of the star, while the wider lower point comes into the centre of the star.
4. Stick the star together by sticking the second point on to the diagonal of the first, and so on (Figure 2c, page 8).

22. Eight-pointed star (Figure 39)

MATERIALS
8 rectangles 4" × 1³/4" (10 × 4.5 cm)

METHOD
For star no. 21 we used pieces 4" × 3" (10 × 7.5 cm). By using narrower pieces such as 4" × 1³/4" (10 × 4.5 cm) with the same folding plan you will get this eight-pointed star.

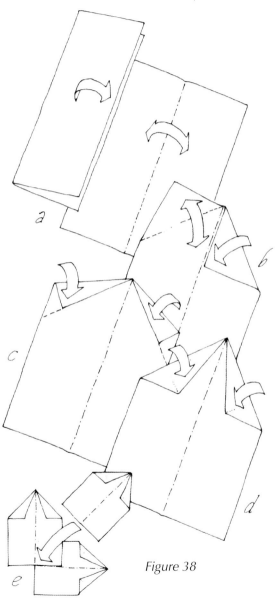

Figure 38

Figure 39

Figure 40

23. Eight-pointed star (Figure 40)

MATERIALS
8 rectangles 4″ × 4″ (10 × 7.5 cm)

METHOD
Fold the pieces over lengthwise and open them up again. Fold the two top corners to the centre-line and open them up again to halve them (Figures 38b–d).

The parts which are not folded come to the centre of the star; first stick four star-points together to make a star with four points (Figure 38e) and then stick the remaining points between the first four.

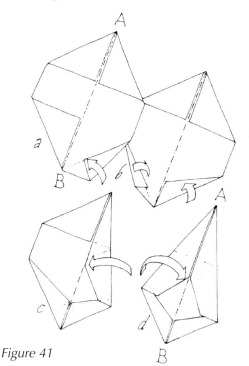

Figure 41

24. Eight-pointed star (Figure 42)

MATERIALS
8 rectangles 4″ × 3″ (10 × 7.5 cm)

METHOD
Fold the pieces as described in stages 1 and 2 of star no. 21, but do not stick down the bottom corners. Open up again the sides of the lower point (which will soon come into the middle of the star) and then fold over the two side-flaps in to the diagonal creases so that a new form is produced (Figure 41).

Then continue with stages 3 and 4.

25. Eight-pointed star (Figure 43)

MATERIALS
8 rectangles 4″ × 3″ (10 × 7.5 cm)

METHOD
Follow stages 1 and 2 of star no. 21. Then open out again the lowest points *E* and *F* (which come into the centre of the star). Carefully fold point *B* to point *D* and point *B* to point *C* so as to determine the middle of the folds *BD* and *BC* (Figure 44a). Fold points *E* and *F* to these points and then fold *BD* and *BC* again to the inside (Figure 44b). Then finish off with stages 3 and 4 of star no. 21 (Figures 44c and d).

Figure 42

Figure 43

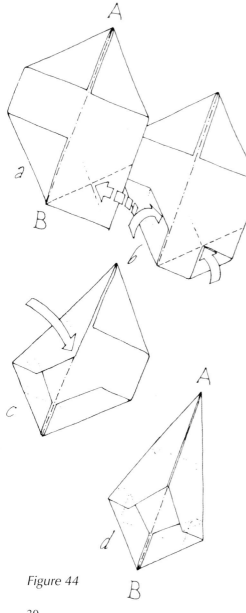

Figure 44

26. Sixteen-pointed star (Figure 45)

MATERIALS
16 rectangles 4″ × 3″ (10 × 7.5 cm)

METHOD
Fold the sixteen points of this star according to stages 1 to 3 of star no. 21.

Continue as follows: First stick two points together as shown in Figure 2c on page 8 and stick the third point between the first two. Stick the fourth point on to the third, and the fifth again between the third and fourth, and so on. Because many layers of paper are folded and stuck over each other it is important to use a light-colored transparent paper.

Figure 45

27. Pointed eight-pointed star (Figure 46)

MATERIALS
8 rectangles 4³/4″ × 1³/4″ (12 × 4.5 cm)
(The diameter of star 9¹/2″, 24 cm)

METHOD
Fold the star-points as described in star no. 21. Because of the narrower shape of the pieces the star-point now appears as in Figure 47a. Make sure that the folds at the top do not come quite to the centre-line. Finally fold the sides from the top point A once more to the centre-line (Figure 47b). Stick the star together in the usual way (Figure 2c on page 8).

Do not make the pieces too small — 4³/4″ × 1³/4″ (12 × 4.5 cm) is the minimum size. Alternatively use 6″ × 1³/4″ (15 × 4.5 cm) pieces.

28. Acute sixteen-pointed star (Figure 48)

MATERIALS
16 rectangles 4³/4″ × 1³/4″ (12 × 4.5 cm)
(The diameter of star 9¹/2″, 24 cm)

METHOD
Fold the star-points in the same way as for star no. 27. Stick the star together as described in star no. 26.

The star which is thus formed resembles the broad sixteen-pointed star (no. 26) of Figure 45, but the pattern of rays stands out rather better.

Figure 47

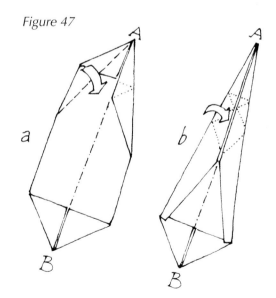

Figure 46

29. Acute sixteen-pointed star (Figure 50)

MATERIALS
16 rectangles 6″ × 1³/₄″ (15 × 4.5 cm)
(The diameter of star 12″, 30 cm)

METHOD
In this star an extra fold is added and so we use a larger size of paper.

Fold the star-points in the same way as described in star no. 21. The result is shown in Figure 47a. Now first fold the sides from the bottom point to the centre-line (Figure 49a). Then fold the sides from the top point to the centre-line (Figure 49b). Stick this star together just like star no. 26. The result is astonishing.

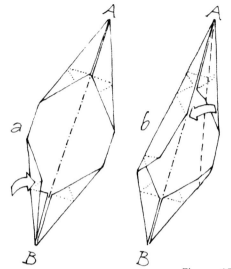

Figure 49

Figure 48

Figure 50